Irene From Petersen

Great Wire Jewelry

Projects and Techniques

LARK BOOKS

Asheville, North Carolina

Editor: Katie DuMont
Art Director and Production: Thom Gaines

Library of Congress Cataloging-in-Publication Data
Peterson, Irene From.
    [Smykker fra Vikingetid, og du selv kan lave. English]
    Great wire jewelry : projects and techniques/
Irene From Peterson.
       p. cm.
    Includes index.
    ISBN 1-57990-093-3
    1. Jewelry making.   2. Wire craft.   I. Title.
TT212.P48.   1999
739.27'028--dc21   98-40919
                                           CIP

10 9 8 7 6 5 4 3 2 1

First Edition

Published by Lark Books
50 College St.
Asheville, NC 28801, US

Originally published in 1997 by Aschehoug Dansk Forlag A/S, as *Smykker fra Vikingetid og Nutid*,
by Irene From Peterson

Distributed by Random House, Inc., in the United States, Canada, the United Kingdom, Europe,and Asia
Distributed in Australia by Capricorn Link (Australia) Pty Ltd., P.O. Box 6651, Baulkham Hills Business
Centre, NSW 2153, Australia
Distributed in New Zealand by Tandem Press Ltd., 2 Rugby Rd., Birkenhead, Auckland, New Zealand

Printed in Hong Kong by Oceanic Graphic Printing Productions Ltd.

ISBN-1-57990-093-3

CONTENTS

FOREWORD

It always feels good when someone admires the jewelry you're wearing. It feels even better when you yourself are the artist. What could be more wonderful than handcrafting your very own jewelry, using authentic Old English designs and techniques?

Throughout history, the wearing of costly ornaments has carried great social significance, revealing power, status, and wealth. Imagine the Viking chieftain and his wife adorned with armbands, collars and chains of the purest gold and silver, while commoners had to be satisfied with amber, glass and clay beads. Indeed, only a fortunate few could don costly and finely-crafted chains.

Many ancient Viking treasures have been unearthed in Scandinavia. I'm still fascinated when I see pieces that, in spite of centuries in the earth or in a bog, are still bright and handsome after just a bit of cleaning.

These historic treasures are, unfortunately, not for us to possess. The good news is we can make our own copies of them and it's not as difficult as it looks! You will need very few tools and all the materials can be readily purchased. Best of all you needn't be as strong as a Viking warrior to make these.

Have fun!
Irene From Petersen

Every project is marked according to degree of difficulty:

 1 Viking = Very Easy - also suited for children

 2 Vikings = Easy

 3 Vikings = A Little Difficult

 4 Vikings = Difficult

---

MATERIALS, OXIDIZING AND POLISHING

All projects in this book have been tested using the directions. Other kinds and weights of wires can be substituted, but to start with, it's safer to follow the directions closely. In each project description, materials (and amounts) are provided and the necessary tools and techniques are described the first time they are introduced.

Types of wire
Silver: Silver is graded according to the amount of silver content and comes in stiff and soft wire. Soft wire is the most useful and the easiest to work with. If you need to make a wire stiffer, you can accomplish this by hitting it with a plastic hammer.

.999 silver: This is pure silver and very soft. Use this quality only if you are skilled in making chains. The wire is difficult to keep even. Available in gauges up to 32 (0.25 mm).

.935 silver: 935 silver is an alloy of 935 parts per 1000 pure silver with about $^{65}/_{1000}$ copper. This quality wire is the easiest to work and you can get a handsome piece even on your first project. Comes in gauges up to 24 (0.5 mm).

.925 SS: Sterling silver is an alloy of 925 parts silver per 1000 and about $^{75}/_{1000}$ copper. Be aware that the wire is a little stiff to work with. Comes in gauges up to 24 (0.5 mm).

Silver plated wire: Copper wire with a very thin coating of silver. This wire is somewhat stiff and isn't good for knitting, but can be used for both braiding and twisting.

German silver wire: An alloy of copper, nickel, and zinc, is not recommended for jewelry making.

Copper wire: Pure copper can be used for all the techniques here. Comes in gauges up to 32 (0.25 mm).

Colored copper wire: Copper wire with a colored surface. It can be used for braiding and twisting, but not for knitting, which may cause the colored surface to flake off. Comes in 30 and 24 gauge (0.35 mm and 0.5 mm) in many colors.

Brass wire: An alloy of copper and zinc, is somewhat harder than silver and copper. Brass wire is best for braiding and twisting and comes in various gauges up to 32 (0.25 mm).

Bronze wire: an alloy of copper, tin and a little zinc, is often very difficult to knit or braid. Comes in gauges up to 28 (0.4 mm).

Oxidizing

Over time, the natural process of oxygen on metal will "oxidize" it, turning the metal a darker shade. One of the oldest and easiest ways to recreate this "antiqued" look is to use liver of sulphur, which can be found in jewelry and bead shops, and supply catalogs. (You might also check with your pharmacist.) This process adds depth to a piece of jewelry, emphasizes its design, and removes the new, raw look from the metal.

Submerge a finished piece of silver jewelry in half a cup of warm water and enough liver of sulphur to turn the water dark brown. The longer it remains in the solution, the darker it will become. Don't let the jewelry stay in the solution for more than an hour. Remove the piece, using plastic tongs and rinse thoroughly. Now, using pulverized pumice, or a nonchlorine abrasive cleanser, you can remove as much of the oxidation as you want, to create the look you desire. Rinse and dry the piece thoroughly.

NOTE: Liver of sulphur smells nasty when used and can burn your skin and clothing, so be careful!

Polishing and care

The most handsome result, without compare, is to tumble polish your silver projects. In a tumbler (actually used for polishing stones), special stainless steel balls (bags of assorted sizes are best) are mixed with a little water and silver (or copper) polish. The pieces should be tumbled 30 minutes to an hour. Use a strainer to empty the tumbler so that the steel balls are not lost in the rinse water. Rinse thoroughly with clean water, and dry with a soft cloth. If one or two little steel balls are trapped in the piece, work them loose with a needle.

Non-oxidized silver can also be cleaned by dipping it in sterling silver cleaner designed for flatware.

Clean copper with a cream copper cleaner, warm water and detergent, or in the polishing tumbler.

Brass is cleaned with cream cleaners designed for yellow metals, warm water and detergent, or in the polishing tumbler. Never tumble brass jewelry with oxidized jewelry of other metals.

CAUTION: *Never polish chains with a polishing machine! Should the chain get caught in the machine, your fingers can be ripped to pieces.*

Knitted, Twisted, and Braided Wire Jewelry

VIKING KNITTING

Finds in Scandinavia have shown that the Vikings had the technology to make chains of both fine and somewhat coarser metal wire. Chains were assembled from many pieces of wire, without the use of solder, into handsome and flexible jewelry.

Metalworking tools recovered from Viking finds are much like those used today. The pliers were more crude, and the drawplates looked more primitive, but their functions were identical to our modern tools.

Working metal wire with *metal* tools makes it stiffer, more brittle, and more susceptible to breakage. Special equipment is needed to anneal the wire (warm it until it glows and becomes soft again) so it can be worked without breaking.

However, this was not a problem for the Vikings, and it need not be for us today! By working with predominantly *wooden*, *leather* and *rubber* tools, annealing is unnecessary. You can copy the old Viking jewelry with very few tools and with an ordinary table as a workspace.

The Viking "knitting" presented here is structurally a looping technique that preceded traditional knitting by centuries and was used by the Vikings not only for jewelry, but also for woolen clothing. The technique consists of backstitching fiber (in this case, wire) in loops, first around a starter and then around earlier rows of stitches, producing something that resembles twisted knit stitches.

Which wire to use
Silver and copper wires are best for Viking knitting. The best gauge is 26 (0.5 mm), which will give you regular, good looking results from the very beginning. If you use wire finer than 28-gauge (0.4 mm), you should place a wire or a leather thong inside the chain to stabilize it.

Wire as heavy as 22-gauge (0.8 mm) can certainly be used, but requires strong hands and more skill.

Most important tools
(See photo on page 59, for reference.)

1 pair flat-nose pliers without ridges
1 pair needle-nose pliers
1 small vise
1 hardwood drawplate (a die plate
   through which wire is pulled to
   reduce its diameter)
Mandrels (an axis, or spindle around
   which wire can be bent)

Starter kits are available with drawplates and mandrels included, but you can easily make these yourself.

Mandrels
Mandrels can be made of knitting needles or Allen wrenches in $3/32$, $1/8$, and $3/16$ inches (2.5, 3.5, and 5 mm).

To make room for the wire when you're knitting, file a little notch about $2/3$ of the way in on the short leg of the Allen wrench. Polish the notch with emery paper.

Drawplate
Make the drawplate from a piece of hardwood, such as oak, maple, or beech, about $5\frac{1}{2}$ inches (14 cm) long, 2-$\frac{1}{2}$ inches (5 cm) wide, and 1 inch (2.54 cm) thick. Bore holes $1/4$ inch (0.5 cm) apart, from 1.5 to 10 mm in diameter.

You have now made your own drawplate, which you will use to draw your finished knitting even and pliable.

GETTING STARTED WITH VIKING KNIT

Startup bundle for single knit, double-knit, and triple knit

Set the mandrel upright in the vise. The notch should be to the left if you are right handed, or the opposite if you're left-handed.

It's a good idea to make the startup bundle in a different color from the actual knitting. Use, for example, about 16 inches (40 cm) colored copper wire for the startup bundle and the first few rows. Change over to the real wire for

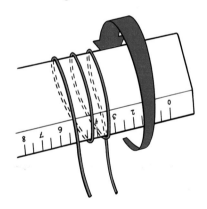

the project only when your stitches begin to lie evenly. You always discard the startup bundle and the starting stitches afterwards, so this will save on your expensive silver wire.

1. Starting at one end about 2¾ inches (7 cm) in and using colored wire, wrap the wire around a ruler, as many times as you want stitches. So, if you want 3 stitches, wind it around 3 times, 4 times for 4 stitches, and so forth.

2. Slip the wire off the ruler and twist the loops together about ⅜ inch (1 cm) from the end that doesn't have loose ends. Wrap the ends around the twist once or twice until they feel like they won't come loose.

3. Spread the loops apart to look like a daisy and pinch the ends of the loops together lightly. These are your startup **loops.**

4. Take a piece of the knitting wire 10-12 inches (25-30 cm) and wrap one end around the twist to anchor it.

5. Place the "flower" over the mandrel, distributing the "petals" evenly to encourage the stitches to lie evenly. The short leg of the mandrel (Allen wrench) should point away from your dominant hand (left if you're right handed, right if you're left handed).

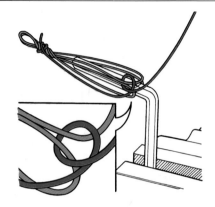

6. Bring the end of the knitting wire over the notch in the mandrel right to left behind the two adjacent sides of two petals, then toward you, drawing the two sides together very loosely. The loop should be crossed above the two startup petals, as shown. Hand-crimp the wire lightly there, then move to the next juncture of petals on the right.

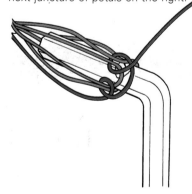

7. Turn the next two startup petals toward you and make another stitch identical to the first. Tighten the wire a little between them. Continue this way until all the startup petals have been "stitched together." Try to keep the spaces between stitches even.

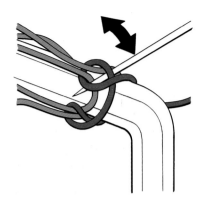

8. When you've gone completely around once, loosen all the stitches carefully with a needle (slide the needle under the stitch and wiggle it carefully). You can also regulate the distance between stitches a little this way. There should be enough space now that you can forget about the startup petals and work only with the knitted stitches. Turn the startup in toward you for the first stitch.

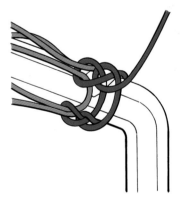

9. Push the knitting wire from the back toward you, going under the entire first stitch. Give a gentle pinch at the top of the stitch you just knitted at the same time you turn the piece, bringing the next stitch toward you. This pinch will help anchor the stitches and keep them even. You may pull a little here, but it's best not to pull too hard at the beginning. As with other knitting, some peo-

ple knit loosely, others tightly. Here it doesn't matter much as long as the stitches and the spaces between them look the same.

Single knit

If you continue as you are knitting now, the result will be single knit. This will be very open and is best suited to the open, rope-like knit shown at upper left on page 11.

Double and treble knit

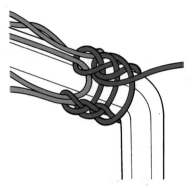

If, after a couple of rounds of single knit, you count back 2 rounds and string the wire through there for your stitch, and continue doing this around, you will be double knitting. Double knitting is the most common knit and produces a handsome, even, and close chain which is still pliable.

If you count back 3 rounds and knit through that, you are double-treble knitting. You will knit very closely and firmly. The chain will be handsome, but a little stiff.

Crooked stitch distribution

If one stitch is too close to the one above it, you can even this out by making a very loose stitch, then tightening those on either side of it a little more than usual. This adjustment won't show after the chain has been drawn through the drawplate.

Joining a new wire

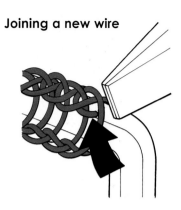

When you run out of wire, clip the wire where it emerges from behind the stitch above, about 1/8 inch (3 mm) from the stitch.

Use the point of your pliers to push the stump in under the stitch as if it were a regular stitch.

Take a new piece of wire about 16 inches (40 cm) long and make a little hook about 1/8 inch (3 mm) in diameter in one end.

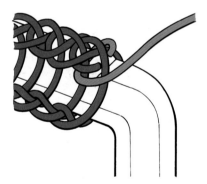

Lead the other end through the stitch as if you were knitting the same stitch all over again, following the path of the first, cut end, but bring the new wire out under the first. Then bring the wire over 2 rounds to the front and across the cut-off end as shown. For double knitting, it may seem that you are going back three rounds instead of 2, but just follow the path of the last stitch. Fasten the little hook at the far end around the wire from the preceding round (as shown) just where the cut end of the old wire points right, so that it is secured to the round between stitches. There is no overlap.

Continue as before, but take care that the hook doesn't slip loose in the first round. If it should pop loose, set it back in place before drawing the chain.

Drawing

Secure the drawplate in the vise. When the chain is as long as you want it (it will gain 20 percent by being drawn), leave a 6-inch (15 cm) piece of the knitting wire hanging. Use this if you find you've made the chain too short: you

can force a small mandrel into the chain again, then a larger one until you have the right size and continue to knit.

(NOTE: This is extremely difficult and a huge bother, so it's better to knit too long, than too short!)

Check all cut ends and beginning hooks to make sure everything is well secured. If anything is loose, push it into place with a needle.

If your knitting is very uneven, slide a knitting needle through it, as thick a one as possible, and roll the chain back and forth on a flat surface between two layers of leather. Do this before drawing the piece. See page 19 for this procedure.

Now you work magic!
Remove the mandrel. Put the bound-together end of your startup loops through the hole in the drawplate that is just the least bit tight, and using flat-nose pliers and gripping only the startup piece, pull the chain through the hole.

Repeat this in a smaller hole, and smaller again. Optionally, pull it through the same hole a couple of times.

When you feel that the chain has stayed firm after being pulled through the same hole twice, it's finished, if it's a necklace. If you pull it through again, you will risk twisting it, and this is nearly impossible to get out again. Bracelets are not as delicate in this respect.

To soften up the knit and make it more pliable, you can run it around a dowel or rod, or old table leg and pull it back and forth a few times. Careful not to scratch the table leg!

To put the knit on a leather thong or a stabilizing wire, remember to insert this into the chain before you draw it, and pull them through together. It's more difficult to put this in later.

Finishing
To finish, nip off the startup and any irregular rounds at the beginning. Work in the cut ends and discard any loose bits, so that only one wire remains at each end.

Now your knitted piece is ready to be mounted with end caps and a clasp.

Twisted knit chain and earrings p. 20

Knitted bracelet on a leather cord p. 12
Twisted knit ring and twisted knit bracelet p. 20

Long chain with cross and coil ends p.13

Oxidized silver bracelet with coil ends p.14

Ring with silver end beads p.16

Knitted necklace w/silver cones p. 12 and ring with silver cones p. 1

Flat bracelet in oxidized silver p. 13

Bracelet in oxidized silver p. 13

Twisted knit bracelet and ring p. 20

Hoop earrings with knit chains p. 16

Bracelet on a leather cord

MATERIALS:
3' 4½" (1 meter) 26-gauge (0.5 mm)
 .935 silver wire
16" (40 cm) leather cord
Photo: page 11

On 3 stitches and a 3.5 mm mandrel, double-knit until the wire is used up. Thread the leather cord through the knit and center the wire knitting on the cord before pulling it through the drawplate. Draw both through at the same time, holding only the startup bundle to avoid damaging the cord. Draw it as many times as you reasonably can.
Nip off the startup bundle and bend loose ends neatly into the knit using the round-nose pliers. Tie the cord with a slip knot.

Leather slipknot

Allow 6 inches (15 cm) of cord for each knot.
Cross the 2 ends at the point where the knot will be when the bracelet is its largest, exactly opposite the center of the knitting, allowing 6 inches (15 cm) on each cut end. Study the drawing of the knot above: Wrap the end over itself and the other end 3 times, working away from the cross point, and stick the end through the wraps. Make an identical knot (going in the opposite direction) with the other end. The length of the bracelet can now be changed by pulling the knots apart or together.

Necklace with cones

FINISHED LENGTH: 16½" (42 cm)
 excluding findings
MATERIALS:
50' 7" (15 m) 26-gauge (0.5 mm)
 .935 silver wire
1' 8" (0.5 m) 20-gauge (1.0 mm)
 silver wire
2 silver cones, 15 mm
1 silver clasp, 13 mm
2 silver jump rings for the clasp
Photo: page 11

Start with 4 stitches mounted on a ³⁄₁₆-inch (5 mm) mandrel and double-knit 14 inches (35 cm) total. When drawing through the drawplate, don't overdo it, or the knit will begin to twist.
Mount the cones and findings.

For a matching bracelet of the same thickness, use about 16' 10½" (5 m) of 26-gauge (0.5 mm) .935 silver wire.

Mounting the cones without glue

1. Pinch the ends of the knit together carefully so that the cones fit down over the ends. Work a hole into the knit ¼ inch (.5 cm) from the end, wide enough to allow a 20-gauge silver wire to pass through.

2. Put the 20-gauge wire through and bend it up against the end of the chain, so the cone can slide down and cover it. Slide the cone over the wire and the end of the chain and press the cone on firmly.

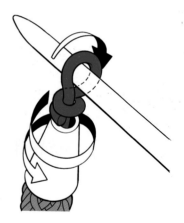

3. Place a No. 3 knitting needle against the end of the cone. Bend the wire around the needle, then around itself once as close to the cone as possible. Nip off the remaining wire and press the end in place with pliers. Straighten the loop up with round-nose pliers.
Mount a cone on the other end the same way.
Mount a jump ring through each loop and a clasp in one of the rings.

Oxidized bracelet

FINISHED LENGTH: 6" (15 cm)
excluding findings
MATERIALS:
16' 10½" (5 m) 26-gauge (0.5 mm)
.935 silver wire
2 silver end caps, 4.2 mm ID (inside
diameter)
1 silver clasp, 11 mm
2 jump rings for the catch
Photo: page 11

Start with 4 stitches on a ⅛-inch
(3.5 mm) mandrel and double-knit about
5 inches (12.5 cm.)
Pull through the drawplate. Check
length. Glue on the end caps.
Oxidize, then polish in a drum tumbler.
(see page 6).

Mounting end caps with glue
A 2-part thick epoxy is best for gluing
metal to metal.
Finish the knit completely and pinch the
ends together lightly where the end
caps will be. A tight fit is best.
Mix the glue according to the directions
on the package and dip the ends of the
knit in the glue. There should be a lot of
glue as some of it will be lost in the knit
itself. Put a little glue in the end caps as
well. Slide them on and turn them so
they face the same way and won't twist
when the clasp is fastened later.
Immediately wipe off excess glue. Let
the glue dry completely before mounting
the jump rings and clasp and oxidizing
the piece (see page 6).

Flat bracelet in oxidized silver

FINISHED LENGTH: 6¾" (17 cm)
without findings
MATERIALS:
16' 10½" (5 m) 26-gauge (0.5 mm)
.935 silver wire
2 silver end caps with a 6 mm ID (inside
diameter)
1 spring catch, 8 mm
Photo: page 11

Starting with 4 stitches on a ⅛-inch
(3.5 mm) mandrel, double-knit 5½ inches (14 cm). Draw through the drawplate
until the chain is tight and the right
length.
Lay the knit on a piece of soft leather.
Now pound it softly with a rubber or
plastic hammer. Try to hit consistently
along the top of two lengthwise lines of
stitches. With a careful hand and a quiet
mind, pound the entire length of the
piece, then turn it over, and pound the
back the same way. Finally, pound it
gently along the sides to even it out.
The results are well worth taking the
time to do this process patiently and
gently. Optionally, flatten the end caps a
little to match the chain.
Glue on the end caps. Wait until the glue
is completely dry before oxidizing the
bracelet (see page 6).

Long chain with cross and coil ends

FINISHED LENGTH: 27½" (70 cm)
MATERIALS:
57' 3" (17 m) 26-gauge (0.5 mm)
.935 silver wire
13½" (0.3 m) 16-gauge (1.5 mm) silver
wire for coil ends
1 jump ring of 16-gauge (1.5 mm)
silver wire
1 cross (We used a museum
reproduction)
Photo: page 11

Start with 3 stitches on a ⅛-inch (3.5
mm) mandrel and double-knit for 23½
inches (60 cm). Draw through the drawplate at most twice through the hole
where you really have to pull to get it
through. It's a shame if the chain begins
to twist from being drawn too energeti-
cally, so do this firmly and carefully.
Coils are a useful way of ending a chain.
The text and the 2 drawings on page 14
show how to mount coils on a chain.
Mount the coil ends. When they are in
place, join them with one jump ring.
Oxidize the chain (see directions, page 6).
Finally, mount the cross.

Mounting the end coils

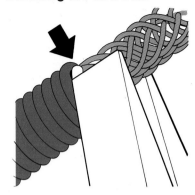

End coils are a practical finish for a chain. These are available purchased, but can also be made by forming a spiral of 16-gauge (1.5 mm) silver wire on a mandrel slightly thicker than the knitted chain. The process is shown on page 30 in the section on ring chains. To harden the coil, pound it with a plastic hammer while it's still on the mandrel.

With nippers, clip off about 1¼ inch (3 cm) of the coil and fit it onto the end of the knitting. Pinch the lowest ring of the coil in toward the knit to bury the end and to anchor it firmly.

Lift the outermost ring on the other end of the coil up and set it upright across the end of the coil, tucking the end in. Do the same with the remaining piece of coil. Mount a clasp on one.

Oxidized silver bracelet with coil ends

FINISHED LENGTH: 6" (15 cm) excluding findings.
MATERIALS:
13' (4 m) 26-gauge (0.5 mm) .935 silver wire
13½" (0.3 m) 16-gauge (1.5 mm) silver wire for the coil ends
1 silver clasp, 13 mm
Photo: page 11

Start with 3 stitches on a ⅛-inch (3.5 mm) mandrel and double-knit about 5½ inches (14 cm). Pull it through the drawplate until it is the right length and thickness.
Mount the coils and the clasp. Oxidize (see page 6).

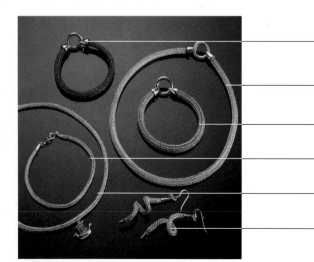

Heavy bracelet in oxidized silver p. 17

Heavy knit silver necklace p. 17

Heavy bracelet in bright silver p. 17

Fine knit silver bracelet p. 17

Fine silver bracelet with pendant p. 16

Corkscrew dangle earrings p. 17

Hoop earrings

MATERIALS:
3' 4½" (1 m) 26-gauge (0.5 mm)
  .935 silver wire
1 pair hoop earrings, 44 mm diameter
Photo: page 11

Start with 3 stitches on a ⅛-inch
(3.5 mm) mandrel. Double-knit until the
wire is used up.
Pull through the drawplate until the knit
is firm. Oxidize and nip off the startup
bundle.
Cut the knitting in two equal lengths and
thread onto the hoops. You may have to
widen the knit a little with a needle if
there isn't enough room for the hoops.
When the knitting is in place, tidy up by
bending the loose wire ends into the knit.

Ring with end beads

MATERIALS:
4' 10½" (1.5 m) 28-gauge (0.4 mm)
  .999 silver wire
4" (10 cm) 20-gauge (1.0 mm) silver
  wire
2 silver end beads with rings (file off
  the rings)
Photo: page 11

Start with 3 stitches on a ³⁄₃₂-inch mandrel and double-knit 2¾ inches (7 cm).
Place the 20-gauge wire inside and pull
the whole assembly through the drawplate, until it's as tight as possible.
Nip off the startup bundle and form into
a ring around a mandrel, dowel, or the
handle of a wooden spoon.

Prepare the end beads by nipping off the
rings. File the raw edges with a file, then
with fine emery paper, then polish in a
drum tumbler. Cut the 20-gauge wire to
size, insert and glue on the end beads.

Ring with cones

MATERIALS:
4' 10½" (1.5 m) 28-gauge (0.4 mm)
  .999 silver wire
4¾" (12 cm) 20-gauge (1.0 mm)
  silver wire
2 silver cones, 6 mm
Photo: page 11

Start with 3 stitches on a ³⁄₃₂-inch mandrel and knit 2¾ inches (7 cm) in dou-
ble-knitting. Slide the 20-gauge wire
through the knit lengthwise and pull the
whole assembly through the drawplate,
making it as tight as possible.
Nip off the startup bundle, but not the
20-gauge wire, which should stick out
about ⅝-inch (1.5 cm) on each end.
Form the ring around a mandrel, dowel
or the handle of a wooden spoon.
Check the length, but don't trim the
heavy wire yet.

Gluing on the cones
Try sliding the cones over the ends of
the knitting. If they don't fit, use flat-
nose pliers to pinch the knit in a little.
When the cones fit, mix epoxy (see page
13), and remove the cones. Be generous
with glue on the ends of the knit, and
replace the cones. Push in hard so that
the cones sit tightly, with the 20-gauge
wire sticking through at both ends. Bend
the ends of the 20-gauge wire over, so
that the cones are held in place under
tension, while the glue dries.
When the glue is completely dry, nip off
the 20-gauge wire as close as possible
to the tip of the cone, then file it off.

Fine silver chain with pendant

FINISHED LENGTH: 14½" (37 cm)
  excluding findings
MATERIALS:
40½" (12 m) 26-gauge (0.5 mm)
  .935 silver wire
2 silver cones with wire spirals, 16 mm
  (see page 12)
1 clasp, 11 mm
1 purchased pendant
1 jump ring
Photo: page 15

Start with 3 stitches on a ³⁄₃₂-inch mandrel and double-treble knit.

When your work is 13½ inches (34 cm)
long, pull it through the drawplate. In
this case, you can draw as much as you
wish, because it's so tightly knit and
short that it can't twist. (On the other
hand, the knit won't change much
because it is so tight already.) Pull the
chain back and forth across a rod, dowel
or the leg of a wooden table to make
the knit more pliable. Mount the pendant on a jump ring large enough to
slide loosely on the chain.

Mount the cones and clasp (see page 12
for directions).

Fine silver bracelet

FINISHED LENGTH: 7½" (18 cm)
excluding findings
MATERIALS:
13' (4 m) 26-gauge (0.5 mm) .935 silver
wire
2 silver cones, 6 mm
1 silver clasp, 9 mm
Photo: page 15

Start with 3 stitches on a ³⁄₃₂-inch mandrel and double-knit.
When work measures about 4¾ inches (12 cm), pull it through the drawplate as much as you can.
Mount cones on the ends (see page 12).

Corkscrew earrings

FINISHED LENGTH: 3½" (9 cm)
MATERIALS:
9' 9" (3 m) 26-gauge (0.5 mm)
.935 silver wire
10" (25 cm) 20-gauge (1.0 mm)
silver wire
4 silver cones, 6 mm
2 silver ear wires
2 silver jump rings
Photo: page 15

Start with 3 stitches on a ³⁄₃₂-inch mandrel and knit about 6 inches (15 cm) in double-knit. This piece will make both earrings.
Slip the 20-gauge wire through the length of the knit and pull the whole assemblage through the drawplate, until it can't be tighter. Be careful not to squeeze the 20-gauge wire out of the knit when drawing.

Nip off the startup bundle, but not the 20-gauge wire.
Tug the 20-gauge wire until the knitting is centered on it.
Divide the knitting in two equal pieces, allowing the heavier wire to protrude from one end of each piece.
Wrap the pieces around a knitting needle, or use your fingers to create a "corkscrew" shape.
Glue the cones in place with the 20-gauge wire poking through the ends.
When the glue is completely dry, use round-nose pliers to bend the 20-gauge wire into a little eye at the top of each earring (see photo, page 12). Mount a jump ring in each eye and the ear wires into the rings.

Heavy silver bracelet

FINISHED LENGTH: 7¾" (19 cm)
excluding findings
MATERIALS:
26' 3" (8 m) .935 silver wire
2 large silver end caps
1 large silver ring clasp, 20 mm
Photo: page 15

This bracelet needs a little extra length because of its thickness.
Start with 5 stitches on a ³⁄₁₆-inch (5 mm) mandrel and double-knit. The stitches are very tightly packed. Be sure they lie densely and evenly from the very beginning or there won't be room around the mandrel.

When the work measures about 6¾ inches (17 cm), slide a knitting needle (U.S. No. 8) through the knitting. Lay this assemblage on a piece

of soft leather, fold the leather over the top and roll the work back and forth inside the leather. You should apply some serious energy to this (see page 19).
When the knitting looks even, remove the knitting needle and pull the knitting through the drawplate's very largest hole once or twice. Don't use a smaller hole. If you wish, you can now oxidize the piece and glue on the end caps afterwards. Remember to be generous with glue. The end caps and the bracelet should be stabilized while the glue is drying.

Heavy silver necklace

FINISHED LENGTH: 16½" (42 cm)
excluding findings
MATERIALS:
65' (20 m) 26-gauge (0.5 mm)
.935 silver wire
2 large silver end caps
Photo: page 15

Start with 5 stitches on a ³⁄₁₆-inch (5 mm) mandrel and double-knit.
Read directions above for the heavy bracelet.
When the work measures 15½ inches (39 cm), follow finishing directions for the heavy bracelet, above.

TWISTED OPEN VIKING KNIT

Twisted knitting is open, single knitting. It's never pulled through a drawplate, so it must be the finished length when the knitting is completed.

Be very meticulous when starting a new piece of wire.

What weight wire?
The best gauge is 26 or 24 (0.5 or 0.6 mm). Finer wire is not suitable for necklaces and bracelets, but may be all right for rings and earrings.

How to even out the twisted viking knit
Remove the mandrel and check all wire changes. Give the hooks a little pinch if they seem to be slipping loose.

Slip a U.S. No. 8 knitting needle (the largest that can fit) through the knit lengthwise. With the needle inside, roll the work between two layers of soft leather as shown (center), while pressing down onto the work surface. The object is to make the chain smooth and even.

Rolling smooth

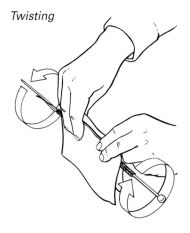

Twisting

How to twist the twisted knit
Find the middle of the knitting and grasp it 1½ - 2 inches (4-5 cm) on each side of the middle, twist one hand forward, the other back.

Change to a U.S. No. 7 knitting needle and twist (in the same directions as before) about 1½ inches (4 cm) out from the first twist.

Continue changing to a smaller knitting needle each 1½ inches (4 cm) until you reach the ends.

This method results in a gentle taper toward the ends, which complements this kind of knitting. Of course, you can twist the entire chain around the same size knitting needle, if you like. (See page 60 for knitting needle conversions.)

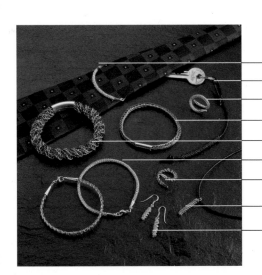

Sinnet tie guard p. 28

Sinnet key ring p. 28

Braided ring p. 22

Copper and silver braided bangle p. 22

Heavy sinnet bangle in silver and copper p. 27

Braided bracelet p. 22

Braided ring p. 22

Sinnet pendant on leather cord p. 28

Sinnet earrings p. 28

Twisted chain

FINISHED LENGTH: 18" (45 cm)
excluding findings
MATERIALS:
32½" (10 m) 26-gauge (0.5 mm)
.935 silver wire
20" (0.5 m) 20-gauge (1.0 mm)
silver wire
2 silver cones, 15 mm
1 clasp
2 jump rings for clasp
Photo: page 11

Start with 4 stitches on a ³⁄₁₆-inch
(5 mm) mandrel and single knit.
Be very careful when starting and
ending wires.
When the work is 18 inches (45 cm),
plus a little extra, twist as described
on p. 19.
Mount cones and clasp (see page 12
for help).

Twisted bracelet

FINISHED LENGTH: 7½" (18 cm)
excluding findings
MATERIALS:
13' (4 m) 26-gauge (0.5 mm) copper
or .935 silver wire
20" (0.5 m) 20-gauge (1.0 mm)
silver wire
2 silver cones, 15 mm
1 silver clasp, 11 mm
2 silver jump rings for clasp
Photo: page 11

Start with 4 stitches on a ³⁄₁₆-inch (5 mm)
mandrel and single knit.
Knit until the work measures the finished
length plus a bit extra, then finish as
described on page 19.
Mount cones and clasp (see page 12).
If you wish to oxidize the bracelet, do
so before mounting the cones and
the clasp.

Twisted earrings

MATERIALS:
9' 9" (3 m) 26-gauge (0.5 mm)
silver wire
2 ear wires
4 jump rings of silver wire, 1 mm
Photo: page 11

Start with 3 stitches on a ⅛-inch
(3.5 mm) mandrel and single-knit until
work measures about 6 inches (15 cm).
Save about 20 inches (½ m) of wire to
"sew" with.

Cut the work in two equal pieces and
twist each piece around a U.S. No. 2
knitting needle. "Sew" the ends together so they feel firm and push loose ends
into the knit. Shape the earrings with
your fingers into teardrops or circles.
In order for the ornaments to dangle
well, string them on 2 jump rings each,
then mount the ear wires through the
top ones.

Twisted ring

MATERIALS:
3' 4½" (1 m) 28-gauge (0.4 mm)
.999 silver wire or copper wire
4" (10 cm) 20-gauge (1.0 mm)
silver wire
2 silver cones, 6 mm
Photo: page 11

Start with 3 stitches on a ³⁄₃₂-inch mandrel and single-knit about 4⅜ inches
(11 cm). Follow finishing directions on
p. 19, but twist the knit around a darning
needle or a U.S. No. 00 knitting needle.
Slip the 20-gauge wire through the knitting lengthwise, letting it stick out ⅜
inch (1 cm) at each end. Pinch the
knitting together at the ends until it fits
smoothly into the cones. Finish by gluing the cones, as described on page 16.

BRAIDS

Silver, copper, colored copper, silvered wire, and brass wire can all be used for the techniques below. Use 22 to 28 gauge (0.35 to 0.8 mm). Heavier wire can be used if you are strong enough to work it!

Note: Wires cannot be added as you proceed, so be sure you have the right length to start.

Braiding technique

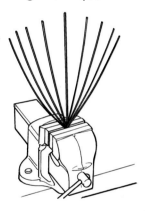

1. Twist the wires together at one end and fasten them firmly in the vise. Arrange the wires with an equal number on both sides of the heavier middle wire. Bend the wires forward so they point toward you, parallel to the floor.

2. Take the outermost left wire, carry it up over the central wire plus two right-hand wires. Bring it down in the center of the right side between 2 wires, then back under 3 wires (including the central wire). It will still be on the left, but will now be the innermost wire, next to the central wire.

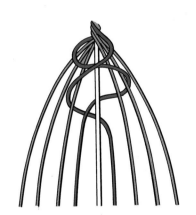

3. Now take the outermost right wire and do the opposite: over the center wire plus two left-hand wires, under the two left-hand wires and the center wire, ending with it as the innermost right wire.

4. Repeat steps 2 and 3 until you have used all the wires once.
Now, take all the right wires in your right hand and all the left wires in your left hand and pull them firmly away from the center. From now on do this after each wire is braided. This assures you a firm and regular braid.

Variation

Try the same braid using two wires as each strand. There will then be two outside wires used in each link of braiding, and the 8 wires will be used as four double strands, but using the same technique. This uses exactly the same amount of wire if you use 26-gauge (0.5 mm) wire. Continue in the same way until you are satisfied with the length.

Finishing braid

Remove the braid from the vise and lay it on a piece of leather. Pound it lightly with a plastic hammer on all 4 sides until the braid is completely even. You can also pull the braid through the drawplate you used for Viking knit.

Nip off the twist at the start and any surplus wires, but don't cut through the central wire if you plan to mount the braid with cones, without using glue (see page 12).

Copper and silver braided bangle

MATERIALS:
8' (2.4 m) 22-gauge (0.8 mm)
  copper wire
8' (2.4 m) 22-gauge (0.8 mm)
  .935 silver wire
1 silver tube, 1¼ inch (3 cm) long,
  with a 7 mm inside diameter
Photo: page 18

There is no center wire in this project.
Divide the wires into 3 copper and 3
silver wires each 32 inches (80 cm) long.
Bend them in half.
Mount these in the vise with 6 copper
wires on one side and 6 silver on the
other. Nip off the ends so they don't
scratch.
Now braid as described on p. 21, but
with no center wire.
When finished, pull through the drawplate if you wish.
File the ends of the tube so they slant
toward each other.

Measure out the right length of braid,
taking care that there is enough to slide
over the thickest part of your hand.
Before mixing epoxy glue, make certain
that all the wires can fit inside the tube.
Remove the tube and apply glue gener-
ously. Clamp the bangle while it dries.
When glue is completely dry, shape the
bangle by hand.

Braided bracelet

FINISHED LENGTH: 5½" (14 cm)
  excluding findings
MATERIALS:
6½' (2 m) 26-gauge (0.5 mm) wire:
  this can be either all .935 silver wire
  or half silver and half copper wire
12" (30 cm) 20-gauge (1.0 mm)
  silver wire
2 silver cones, 6 or 11 mm
1 silver clasp
2 silver jump rings for the clasp
Photo: page 18

Cut the 26-gauge wire in 4 pieces, each
20 inches (50 cm). Bend these in half

so you have 8 ends. Mount these in the
vise with the 20-gauge wire in the center, the other wires with 4 to a side. If
working with 2 metals, put the 4 copper
on one side, the 4 silver on the other.
Braid and finish the bracelet as
described on page 21.
Mount the cones as described on p. 12.

Braided ring

FINISHED LENGTH: 4" (10 cm)
MATERIALS:
3' 4½' (1 m) 26-gauge (0.5 mm)
  .935 silver wire
5" (12 cm) 20-gauge (1.0 mm)
  silver wire
2 silver cones, 6 mm
Photo: page 18

Cut the 26-gauge wire in 4 pieces, each
10 inches (25 cm).
Bend them in half to make 8 ends.
Place these and the 20-gauge silver
wire in a vise with the 20-gauge wire in
the center and braid as described on
page 21. Finish and glue on the cones
(see page 16).

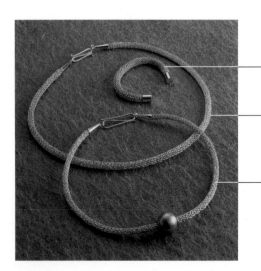

Knit bracelet p. 26

Knitted necklace p. 26

Knit choker with bead p. 26

KNIT ON 3 NAILS

Chains knitted on nails look more knitted than those made with Viking knit. While they aren't as firm or strong as Viking knitted chains, the technique has other possibilities. You can, for example, make chains with a greater circumference. On the other hand, if you make a bracelet with this technique, it must be supported inside to keep it from being flattened when worn.

Which wire is best?
.935 silver wire and copper wire, starting at 28 gauge (0.4 mm). Again, the best is 26-gauge (0.5 mm).

Tools

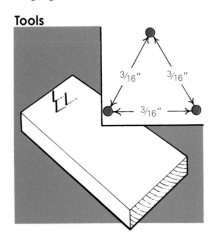

A wooden block with 3 nails
A crochet hook, metric number 1 or 1.25
A wooden drawplate like the one used for Viking knit (see pages 7 and 10.)

How to make your jig, a block with 3 nails
a block of wood, preferably hardwood, about 2 x 4" (4 x 8 cm). Scraps are fine.
3 small brads
2 component epoxy

Measure a triangle on the block as shown, with 3/16 inch (4 mm) separating the points. Bore holes at each point with a 1 mm bit, straight down. Mix 2-part epoxy and squeeze some into the holes. Tap in the brads. Wipe away excess glue immediately. When the glue is entirely dry, nip off the heads and file them smooth, so they don't scratch or snag. It is on these nails that the knit stitches are formed.

Getting started

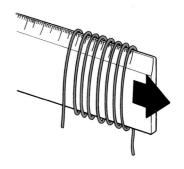

The startup bundle and the first few stitches are always discarded, so save your silver wire for the real thing.

1. Use a piece of colored copper wire about 40½" (1 m) long. Starting a little ways into the length, wind 8 loops over a ruler. (These will be on the side away from the ends of the wire.)

Wiggle the copper wire off the ruler, give the "back end" a solid twist, and wrap the loose ends firmly around the bundle.

2. Spread out the loops to form a daisy.

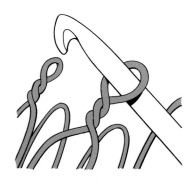

3. Holding onto the fastened end, use the crochet hook to form an eye at the end of each loop by inserting the crochet hook well into a loop, then twisting it in the loop two turns. (More turns could break the wire.)

Stitching

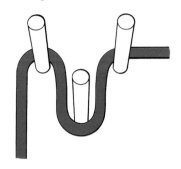

Now take your knitting wire (or a practice piece) and your nail block. Starting from the left about 4 inches (10 cm) in from one end of the wire, bring the wire over the left nail, under the center nail and over the right nail. Lift this off and shift the wire to the left, putting what was on the right nail on the left nail and running the wire under and up again. Try making about 24 stitches. When you have done this, you will simply continue the same way, making more on the same wire.

Starting

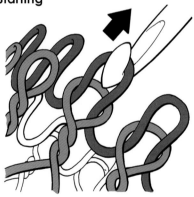

Now, wrap the knitting wire around the twisted eyes of the startup bundle, so that the stitches are outside the eyes.

Push the crochet hook through an eye and catch a stitch. Pull it through the eye and up a little so that the stitch is locked in place. Turn the work to the left (counterclockwise) to the next stitch and repeat. The first round of stitches may pop out a little, but just put them back in again.

When you have 8 stitches knitted, shape them into a circle. Knit the next stitch into the first stitch of the first round. Catch a new stitch through the old first stitch and continue around in this way.

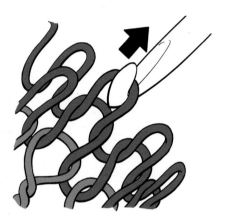

Changing wires

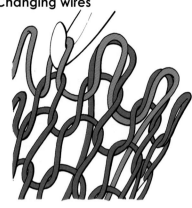

If you run out of wire, add a new one. Let about ¾ inch (2 cm) of the old wire drop down inside the knit. Make a row of stitches on a new wire, also about ¾ inch (2 cm) from the end. Start 2 stitches before the end of the old wire, sliding ¾ inch (2 cm) of the new wire under the knit as shown above, and overlapping the first 2 stitches of the new wire over the last 2 stitches of the old wire. This won't show much on the finished object. Loose ends are not trimmed closely, and up to ⅜ inch (1 cm) can hang down inside the knit.

Drawing

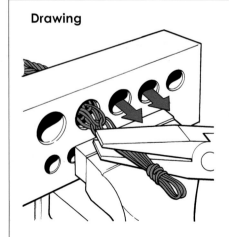

When the chain is completed (about ⅕ less length than the finished measurement), check the points where you changed wires to be sure they are firm and lie nicely. Now mount the drawplate in the vise. Use flat-nosed pliers to pull and always pull only on the startup bundle.

If you have knitted a wide piece with 15 or more stitches, you will have to bore larger holes (15 - 20 mm) in the drawplate.

First pull the work through the large hole once or twice, then through a hole a little smaller. This stabilizes the knit. Don't draw it through too many holes, however, or the knitting will become too stiff.

S-catch

A big S-catch works well for necklaces, but not as well for bracelets.
S-catches can be purchased, but you can easily make a handsome one yourself.
For a 1¼ inch (3 cm) long S-catch, use 4 inches (10 cm) 16-gauge (1.5 mm) silver wire.

With round-nose pliers, bend down one-third of its length.
Bend down the other end in the opposite direction so that the bends are the same length.

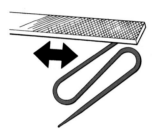

File the ends a little to make the wire narrower.

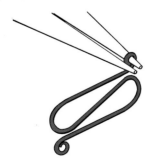

With fine round-nose pliers, bend a little curl in each end to finish.

Now to harden the metal, lay the catch in a piece of leather and pound it with a plastic hammer.
Polish the catch with metal polish or put it in a drum tumbler with steel balls. See page 6 for more detail.

Knit necklace

FINISHED LENGTH: 20" (51 cm)
exluding findings
MATERIALS:
50' 7" (15 m) 26-gauge (0.5 mm) .935 silver wire
20" (0.5 m) 20-gauge (1 mm) silver wire
2 silver cones, 15 mm
6" (15 cm) 16-gauge (1.5 mm) silver wire for S-catch
Photo: page 23

Start with 8 stitches and knit 16½ inches (42 cm) using the basic pattern on pages 24-25.
Pull the work carefully through the drawplate using only the largest holes. Draw until the chain is even and smooth. It should be drawn only until the knit can no longer be pushed together easily. Cut off the startup bundle and mount the cones as described on page 12. Make and attach an S-catch.

Knit choker with bead

FINISHED LENGTH: 16" (40 cm)
excluding findings
MATERIALS:
40½' (12 m) 26-gauge (0.5 mm) .935 silver wire
20" (0.5 m) 20-gauge (1 mm) silver wire
2 silver cones, 15 mm
4" (10 cm) 16-gauge (1.5 mm) silver wire for S-catch
1 purchased bead
Photo: page 23

Start with 8 stitches and knit about 15 inches (38 cm) using the basic pattern on pages 24-25.
Pull through the drawplate until the knit is firm enough.
Slide the bead on first, then mount the cones (see page 12). Make and attach an S-catch.

Knit bracelet

FINISHED LENGTH: 6" (15 cm)
MATERIALS:
16' 10½" (5 m) 26-gauge (0.5 mm) .935 silver wire
6" (15 cm) 14-gauge (2.0 mm) silver wire
6¾" (17 cm) clear plastic tubing (aquarium supplies, etc.) about ¼ inch (0.5 cm) outside diameter.
2 cup style end caps with 7 mm inside diameter (ID)
Photo: page 23

Start with 8 stitches and knit 5 inches (13 cm) using the basic pattern on pages 24-25.
Slide the plastic tubing into the knit and pull the whole assemblage through the drawplate, until it is smooth and even. Now, shape the heavy 14-gauge (2.0 mm) wire around a mandrel or a wooden table leg to the shape you want the finished bracelet to have. When it's the right shape, hammer it with a plastic hammer to make it harder, so it will keep its shape inside the finished bracelet. Now, work the wire into the plastic tubing, which is coated with the silver knit. This can be a little tricky, so work patiently.
Cut off the startup bundle now.
Cut the plastic tubing, the knit, and the thick wire so they are all the same length, pinch the ends a little until the end caps will fit on nicely. Mix 2-part epoxy and glue on the end caps.

CROWN SINNET BRAIDING

For this technique, you can use the same kinds and weights of wire used for regular braiding.
You can braid 3, 4, 5, 6, or 7 wires together into a sinnet.

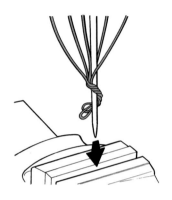

1. Measure wires in the given lengths, twist them together to secure them, and wrap them around a knitting needle, as shown.

Secure the knitting needle and the wires together in a vise. You will work up the needle. Spread the wires around the needle as shown.

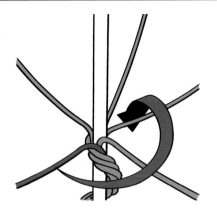

2. Starting with any wire, bring it in a counterclockwise direction over 2 other wires. Bend it down a little at a diagonal, as close as possible to the knitting needle.

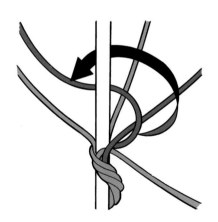

3. Now take the wire directly behind the one you just moved and bring it over the next two wires (including the one you just moved). Repeat this step until you are finished.

Finishing

Roll the sinnet in a piece of leather while pressing down on the work surface (see page 19). Keep the knitting needle inside as you do this.

If the sinnet still seems uneven, pound it a little with a plastic hammer, still without removing the knitting needle. You may have trouble getting the knitting needle out again, but wrapping a piece of leather around the sinnet will help you get a better grip.

Measure the amount you need, then cut off the startup twists first, measure again, and cut off the other end. Turn the cut ends into the sinnet using small round-nose pliers, so they won't snag or scratch.

Heavy sinnet bangle

MATERIALS:
8' (2.4 m) 22-gauge (0.8 mm) copper wire (3 pieces each 32" (80 cm))
10' 8" (3.2 m) 22-gauge (0.8 mm) .935 silver wire (4 pieces each 32" (80 cm))
1 curved silver tube with 10 mm inside diameter
1 U.S. No 10.5 knitting needle
Photo: page 18

Braid around the needle as described on this page until the wire is used up or the bangle is long enough. Finish the piece.

Check the length, remembering that the widest part of your hand must be able to pass through. (The finished bangle doesn't open.) Glue on the tubing, taking care that the sinnet meets in the middle of the tube. Stabilize the bangle while the glue dries. When the glue is completely dry, shape the bangle to its final form.

Earrings and sinnet pendant

Two earrings
MATERIALS:
3' 4½" (1 m) 28-gauge (0.4 mm)
   .999 silver wire (Cut 4 pieces each
   8" (20 cm) long and save the rest
   for sewing.)
2 silver jump rings, 1 mm
2 silver ear wires
Photo: page 18

Pendant on leather cord
MATERIALS:
40½" (1 m) 28-gauge (0.4 mm)
   .999 silver wire (Cut 4 pieces, each
   8" (20 cm) long. Save remainder
   for sewing.)
40½" (1 m) leather cord
Photo: page 18

Twist the wire around a hatpin or other fine long pin and secure the assemblage in a vise.
Braid as described on page 27.
When the sinnet is finished, cut it in two for earrings, (keep it whole for the pendant) and turn in the ends.
Put the remaining wire through the sinnet lengthwise and secure it by sewing into one end. Nip off the wire at one end and bend it into the sinnet so it doesn't scratch or snag. At the other end form a little eye around a needle, as you did when mounting cones without glue (See page 12).
For the pendant, when shaping the eye, remember that the lacing must be able to pass through it loosely. Knot the ends of the laces as shown on p. 12.
For the earrings, mount the jump rings in the two eyes, then the ear wires in the jump rings.

Sinnet tie guard

MATERIALS:
4' 2" (1.25 m) 28-gauge (0.4 mm)
   .999 silver wire (pure silver)
Cut 5 pieces 10" (25 cm).
20" (0.5 m) 20-gauge (1.0 mm)
   silver wire
2 silver cones, 6 mm
a fine (U.S. No. 00) knitting needle
Photo: page 18

Tie guard hanger
Using round-nose pliers and the 20-gauge wire, form the hanger following the drawing below. Nip off the excess. Lay the hanger inside a piece of leather and pound it lightly with a plastic hammer to make it stiffer.

Braiding the sinnet
Place the five wires, twisted together at the bottom, around a fine knitting needle, clamp in a vise and braid as shown on page 27. Thread the rest of the 20-gauge wire through lengthwise. Adjust the length of the sinnet. Mount a cone on each end following directions on p. 12.

Tighten the sinnet so that it curves a little, mount it on the hanger, and finally shape it to perfection with your fingers.

Sinnet key ring

MATERIALS:
4' 2" (1.25 m) colored copper wire
   (5 pieces each 10" (25 cm))
1 heavy leather lace
1 key ring
1 U.S. No. 4 knitting needle
Photo: page 18

Follow the general directions on p. 27 to braid the sinnet.
Remove the knitting needle and thread the leather through the sinnet.
Nip off parts at either end that look messy. Use round-nose pliers to turn all ends into the sinnet, so they don't snag or scratch.
Tie an overhand knot in one end of the lace. Put the key ring on the lace and tie a single leather knot as shown on page 12.

Jewelry from Rings

MAKING AND JOINING RINGS

In Viking times, chains were made of rings in simple 2-in-2 or 3-in-3 patterns. Viking chain mail is the model for today's flat chain mail jewelry. We don't know exactly where all the other patterns come from, but we do know that they come from many different people, who each discovered a new pattern, either on purpose or by accident. They are all extremely handsome!

It's easy to get started
You won't need many tools, only:

2 small flat-nose pliers without ridges
1 helping needle—darning needle or the like
1 piece of string or wire as a holder—26-gauge (0.5 mm) copper wire is fine
a lot of rings and some catches or clasps (Catches and Clasps are mounted directly on the chains, without end caps or glue.)

This is all you actually need to make these wonderful chains.

Most of the drawings show the rings in two different colors. It will be easier to follow the directions if, the first time you make a pattern, you use rings in two different metals.

Jump rings can be purchased in a variety of sizes in copper, brass, and silver. Be aware, however, that there is an important relationship between pattern, wire gauge, and the internal diameter (ID) of the rings. In other words, you can't use the same rings for everything.

The degree of difficulty marked on the patterns is figured, in part, according to whether you make your own rings or use purchased rings. Making your own rings is a little more work and is described later in this section. Also, you'll find information on how to adapt our patterns to different wire gauges and ring sizes.

What wire to use?
.925 or .935 silver wire, copper, brass, and bronze wire in weights from 26 to 14-gauge (0.5 to 2 mm). Heavier wire is very difficult to work with. The most commonly used is 20-gauge (1.0 mm) wire. Also, check the chart on page 60.

Finishing
You can find information on finishing metal jewelry on page 6. You will want to polish these ringed chains in a drum tumbler, which smoothes out any unevenness in assembling and sawing.

Assembling the rings
Learning to close and assemble the rings properly is extremely important, both to prevent scratches and to keep them from popping open again in use.

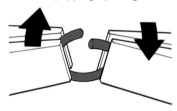

1. Take hold of the ring between two pliers. Gently pull the ends in the direction of the arrows. Open only as much as is necessary and never pull the ends apart horizontally.

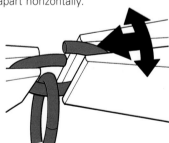

2. To close the ring again, bring the ends toward the middle, just past closed, then back, (so that the two ends meet with some pressure). Wiggle them back and forth until the ring is completely and neatly closed.

Never pinch the ring across its diameter. This will only force it out of shape and make it oval.

Key Numbers & Inside Diameters

All chains have a relationship between the pattern used, the gauge of the wire, and the inside diameter (ID) of the rings. The mandrel (the spindle around which the rings are formed) determines the inside diameter of the rings.

The relation between the gauge of the wire and the (ID) inside diameter is called the "key number".

You won't need key numbers if you are working with one of this book's many pre-calculated patterns. However, by using different key numbers you can create finer or more robust chains from the same patterns. If you want to change the wire gauge of a project, refer to the chart on page 60.

Making your own rings

Manufactured rings are available in many sizes, but why not learn to saw your own rings.

Tools

1 mandrel in the size that matches your project (Mandrel = ID). Metal knitting needles make great mandrels. See page 60 for Knitting Needle Coversion Chart.
1 hand drill; the "egg beater" variety is best.
1 bench vise
1 saw—specially designed for work with silver
Hacksaw blades for metal. Buy a few; they break easily.
1 saw board
1 C-clamp

Making the spiral

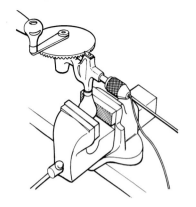

1. Secure the drill handle in the vise. Insert one end of the wire you're using (use about 20 inches) and the mandrel together in the drill's chuck.

2. Very carefully turn the drill, which will turn the mandrel. Hold the wire taut below the mandrel, so that a very tight spiral of wire winds onto the mandrel. Be careful of your fingers toward the end. The wire will try to whip back when you let go.

There are advantages to winding the spiral with 2 wires simultaneously—the rings will be open when they're sawed off, but winding evenly and tightly with two is a little harder.

Sawing the spiral

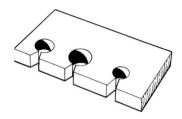

3. Make a sawing board: In a board about 8 inches (20 cm) long, 3¼ inches (8 cm) wide and about ¾ inch (2 cm) thick, bore a couple of holes the spirals will fit through. Cut a notch in from the edge to each hole. Clamp the board to a work surface with the C-clamp, with the holes extending over the edge of the table.

4. Place a blade in the saw. The teeth should point in the direction shown in the drawing. Secure the saw (in the vise, for example) while you tighten the blade. If it's set properly, the blade should make a clinging sound when plucked with a finger.

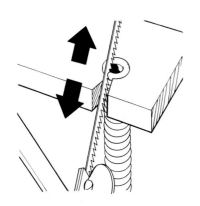

5. Push the spiral up through the hole in the sawing board until the end is level with the board. Hold the saw so that you can make even, soft, completely vertical strokes. Try not to slip and scratch the metal. This will take some time, so focus your attention and be patient.

Twisted rings

Twisted rings look particularly attractive when mixed with smooth rings. However, avoid putting them alone near the clasp, as they lack the strength of smooth rings.

Mount a hook in the drill chuck and secure the drill in the vise as shown. Loop about 40 inches (1 m) of wire over the hook. Turn the drill, while holding the two ends of the wire firm and straight with flat-nose pliers. (This will be much easier if you have someone help you.) It's imperative that the wire be held quite taut while being twisted. Turn until the wire snaps, which will happen near the hook.

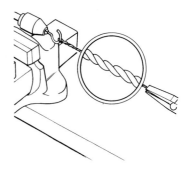

Now use the twisted wire to make a spiral and saw the spiral into rings.

CROSS-LINKED CHAIN

Key number: 3 or 3.5

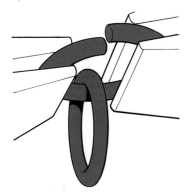

1. Join the rings in pairs, for example, 20 rings joined 2 by 2.

2. Lay them out on the work surface so that the top ring of each pair is turned in the same direction.

3. Now link the pairs together into a chain using single rings of the same size.

Necklace with cross

FINISHED LENGTH: 16½" (42 cm)
excluding clasp

MATERIALS:
43 g rings in 18-gauge (1.2 mm) wire,
  4 mm ID
1 clasp
1 pendant (This is a replica of a cross
  from around 1000 AD from the
  National Museum in Copenhagen),
  with a jump ring, which will be hung
  directly from the clasp.

Photo: page 33

Assemble the chain according to the
directions for a Cross-linked Chain on
the preceding page.

3-IN-3 CHAIN

Key number: 4

This chain—minus the twisted center
rings—is modeled after one from 1500
A.D. made of brass wire and hanging in
National Museum in Copenhagen.

2. String these on string or wire holder
with the twisted ring in the center.

3. Into these rings, set the next 3 rings,
once more with a twisted ring in the
center, and continue.

1. Neatly close 1 twisted and 2 smooth
rings.

— Cross-linked neck chain with cross p. 32
— Single flower chain bracelet p. 34
— Hoop earrings with double flowers p. 35

— Brass double flower chain necklace p. 35

— Bracelet with elephant clasp—3-in-3 chain p. 34
— Copper double flower dangle earrings p. 35

— Copper neck chain with double flowers p. 35

Bracelet with elephant clasp

FINISHED LENGTH: 6¾″ (17 cm)
excluding findings

MATERIALS:
11 g silver rings made of 22-gauge
(0.8 mm) wire, 3.5 mm ID
3 g silver twisted rings made of
26-gauge (0.5 mm) wire, 2 mm ID
1 elephant clasp, which will be mounted
directly on 3 rings.
Photo: page 33

Assemble according to the basic 3-in-3 chain pattern on page 32.

SINGLE FLOWER CHAIN

Key number: 3.5

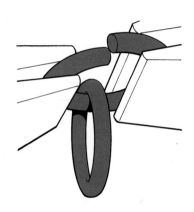

The flower
1. Open one ring slightly and put a closed ring into it.

2. Place them on your work surface, as close together as possible. Put one more ring through both of these rings. When the 3 assembled rings are pushed together on the table, they look a little like a 3-petaled flower.

3. Make about 10 of these flowers.

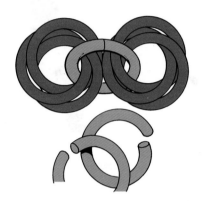

Assembling the flower chain
Open a couple more rings. Place the flowers on the work surface so the rings face the same way and join the rings with a single ring the same size.

Single flower chain bracelet

FINISHED LENGTH: 6½″ (16 cm)
excluding clasp
MATERIALS:
16 g silver jump rings of 18-gauge
(1.2 mm) wire, 4 mm ID
1 heart clasp
Photo: page 33

Assemble following the basic pattern above.

DOUBLE FLOWER CHAIN

Key number: 5

Use the same procedure as the single flower chain, but when making the flowers, use 2 rings every time you used 1 in the single chain. The flowers are still linked by single rings, however.

Brass necklace

FINISHED LENGTH: 16½″ (42 cm)
  excluding clasp
MATERIALS:
35 g brass rings of 20-gauge (1.0 mm)
  wire with a 5 mm ID
1 brass clasp, 13 mm
Photo: page 33

Assemble the chain following the double flower chain pattern described above.

Hoop earrings

MATERIALS:
1 pair silver hoop earrings about 27 mm
  in diameter
14 brass rings of 20-gauge (1.0 mm)
  wire, 5 mm ID

Assemble 2 double flowers
String 1 ring through each flower and
suspend the flower from the earring.

Copper necklace

FINISHED LENGTH: 18″ (45 cm)
  excluding clasp
MATERIALS:
35 g rings in 20-gauge (1.0 mm) wire,
  5 mm ID
1 copper clasp, 13 mm
Photo: page 33

Assemble 11 double flowers and lay them on the work surface, ready to use.

1. Set plain rings together 2-in-2 nineteen times (38 rings) and put a double flower on the last 2 rings.

2. After the flower, 7 times (14 rings) 2-in-2, then the next flower. Repeat this step two more times.

3. After the last flower of step 2, link 3 times (6 rings) 2-in-2, then a flower. Repeat this step two more times.

4. The middle of the chain is between the last 2 flowers. Hang a pendant here of 5 times 2-in-2 rings with a double flower at the bottom.

5. Reverse direction, repeating Step 2, then Step 1. Mount the clasp on the last 2 rings.

Copper dangle earrings

MATERIALS:
2 silver ear wires
28 copper rings of 20-gauge (1.0 mm)
  wire with 5 mm ID
Photo: page 33

Assemble 2 double flowers
To each flower, attach four 2-in-2 rings.
Mount the ear wires in the last 2 rings.

FLAT CHAIN MAIL

Key number: 3.5

This linkage pattern is the same as that used for genuine chain mail armor. Look for it the next time you visit a museum with medieval exhibits.

Lay the chain out flat on a work surface while assembling it so you can see that all the rings face the right way.

1. Join 2 red + 1 blue + 2 red + 1 blue + 2 red. Spread this out on the work surface as shown.

2. Link 1 blue through each of the lower pairs of red rings. Lay the work out on the work surface.

3. Link the 2 lower blues with one red in the center, and 1 red through each blue on the sides.

4. Repeat steps **2** and **3**.

Silver necklace with pendant

FINISHED LENGTH: 16″ (40 cm) excluding clasp and pendant
MATERIALS:
68 g silver rings of 20-gauge (1.0 mm) wire, 3.5 mm ID
1 purchased opal pendant
1 clasp, 9 mm
Photo: page 39

Assemble according to the basic pattern at left. Narrow each end of the necklace to a single jump ring. Attach the opal pendant to one of the single rings. On the other single ring, attach the clasp. You can now "lock" your necklace.

Heavy silver bracelet

FINISHED LENGTH: 6¾″ (17 cm) excluding clasp
MATERIALS:
100 g silver rings of 14-gauge (2.0 mm) wire, 7 mm ID
1 silver ring clasp, 20 mm
Photo: page 39

Assemble according to the basic pattern, ending with 2 rings, and then a single ring, so there is a single ring to link to the clasp.

Silver earrings

FINISHED LENGTH: 1⅝″ (4 cm)
MATERIALS:
9 g silver rings of 22-gauge (0.8 mm) wire, 2.8 mm ID.
2 silver ear studs
Photo: page 39

Assemble according to the basic pattern at left.
Start in the middle (of the side) and build one side at a time.
Join 1 + 2 + 1 + 2 + 1 + 2 + 1 + 2 + 1 + 2 + 1 + 2 + 1 + 2 + 1 + 2 + 1 rings, laying the chain out as you work. Be sure everything's pointing the right way. With the chain laid out correctly on the table, work along one edge: where two rings lie over each other, connect them with another ring, matching the direction to the ring beside it in the same row. Each edge ring will get 2 new rings connecting it to the ring above and the ring below. Continue to do this along one side, going back and forth, with one less ring in each row, until you reach a point with only 1 ring.
Repeat this on the other side, then set a single ring and the ear stud in the point on a lengthwise end.

ROUND CHAIN MAIL

Key number: 3.5

1. Connect 2 red rings to 1 blue to 2 red to 1 blue to 2 red rings, and connect the 2 sides with 1 blue ring. All the rings of the same color will lie in the same direction.

2. Lay them out on your work surface. Thread a piece of wire loosely through the top 3 red rings. Hold onto the wire and turn upside down.

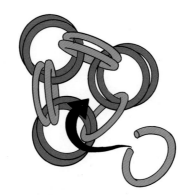

3. Now gather the (new) top set of 3 red rings from inside the blue rings and link them with 3 blue rings where they meet.

4. Gather the blue rings from outside the red rings and link them with red rings where they meet.

Repeat steps **3** and **4** to make the chain.

New rings are always inserted into the rings most recently added.

Silver bracelet

FINISHED LENGTH: 7½″ (18 cm) excluding clasp
MATERIALS:
41 g rings of 20-gauge (1.0 mm) wire and 3.5 mm ID
1 ring clasp, 15 mm
2 jump rings in 16-gauge (1.5 mm) wire, 5 mm ID
Photo: page 39

Assemble according to the basic pattern. Join the last 3 rings at each end to 2 rings and then to the heavier ring, to which the clasp is attached.

OPEN ROUND CHAIN MAIL

Key number: 4

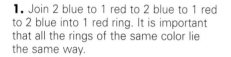

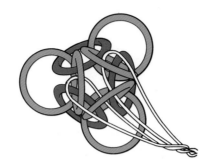

1. Join 2 blue to 1 red to 2 blue to 1 red to 2 blue into 1 red ring. It is important that all the rings of the same color lie the same way.

2. Lay the rings on the work surface and thread a string or wire loosely through the uppermost blue rings.

3. Lift up on the string so that the rings hang down.
Gather the 3 rings hanging farthest down and link them 2 by 2, where they meet, with 3 red rings.

Repeat step **3** continuously.
Always link the rings most recently added.

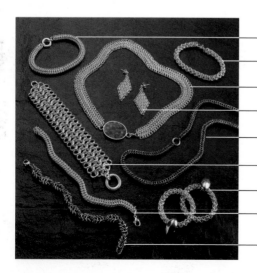

Round chain mail silver bracelet p. 37

Open round chain mail bracelet p. 40

Silver flat chain mail necklace with pendant p. 36

Silver flat chain mail earrings p. 36
Long Queen's chain in oxidized silver p. 41

Heavy flat chain mail bracelet in silver p. 36

Silver, open round chain mail clip-back earrings p. 40

Queen's chain silver bracelet p. 41

Segmented Queen's chain bracelet in oxidized silver p. 41

Silver bracelet

FINISHED LENGTH: 7½" (18 cm)
excluding clasp
MATERIALS:
22 g silver rings of 20-gauge (1.0 mm)
wire with 4 mm ID
1 clasp
Photo: page 39

Assemble according to the basic pattern on page 38.

Join the final rings of the pattern with 2 rings, then with 1, and attach the clasp to that.

Silver clip-back earrings

MATERIALS:
2 purchased silver hoop earrings
(designed for pierced ears. They will be hidden inside the ring.)
2 purchased silver clipback earrings
(with room for the chain in the decorative portion.)
20 g rings of 22-gauge (0.8 mm) wire
with 3 mm inside diameter
Photo: page 39

Assemble following basic pattern on page 38.

Assemble a chain long enough to cover the hoop earring. Open the hoop earring and work the chain onto it. Close the earring and work the chain a little.
If the chain doesn't reach, add more links until it does. Connect the chain together at the end so that the pattern matches all the way around.

Make another.

QUEEN'S CHAIN

Key number: 4

1. Close two red rings and thread a wire or string through them. Attach 2 blue, then 2 red to these as shown.

2. Turn the two last red rings backward and out of the way. Part the two blue rings and insert 2 blue rings in between them.

3. In the 2 blue rings, put 2 red rings. Repeat steps 2 and 3.

You will always be placing rings in the most recently added rings.

NOTE: This particular chain has a tendancy to twist. It's helpful to lay it on your work surface and flatten with your fingers, as needed.

Silver bracelet

FINISHED LENGTH: 7½" (18 cm)
MATERIALS:
26 g rings of 20-gauge (1.0 mm) wire, 4 mm ID
1 clasp, 13 mm, set directly on the final rings
Photo: page 39

Assemble following the pattern at left.

Long chain in oxidized silver

FINISHED LENGTH: 23" (58 cm)
excluding clasp
MATERIALS:
55 g silver rings in 22-gauge (0.8 mm) wire, 3.5 mm ID
1 ring in 14-gauge (2.0 mm) wire, 7 mm ID
Photo: page 39

Assemble according to the basic pattern at left.
Try not to be too rough on the rings. Attach the two ends of the finished chain together with the heavier ring. Finally, oxidize the chain (see page 6).

Segmented bracelet in oxidized silver

Key number 3.75
(NOTE: This is not the original key number and can only be used when the chain is divided into segments, as here.)

FINISHED LENGTH: 7½" (18 cm)
excluding clasp
MATERIALS:
35 g silver rings of 18-gauge (1.2 mm) wire with 4.5 mm ID
20 twisted rings made from 3' 4½" (1 m) of 24-gauge (0.6 mm) wire twisted, then wound onto a 4.5 mm mandrel (see pages 30-31)
1 silver clasp, 11 mm
Photo: page 39

A segment is comprised of 14 rings assembled according to the basic pattern.

Assemble 10 segments.

Connect the segments with 2 twisted and 1 smooth rings. End with a twisted and a smooth in each end.
Mount the clasp on one of the smooth rings.
Oxidize the bracelet (see page 6).

CRISS-CROSS CHAIN

Key number: 4

1. Close 1 red ring and place it on a string or wire. In this ring, place a blue ring and another red ring through both, at right angles to both.

2. Set a blue ring through the cross and through the first red ring—that is to say, through all 3 rings.

3. Lay the chain flat and turn it a half turn in toward yourself so the last 2 rings appear cross and the first blue ring pops up. Set the next ring through these last three rings.

Repeat step **3**.

Silver bracelet with ball clasp

FINISHED LENGTH: 7½" (18 cm)
excluding clasp

MATERIALS:
17 g silver rings of 20-gauge (1.0 mm) wire, 4 mm ID
2 rings of 18-gauge (1.2 mm) wire, 4 mm ID to support the clasp
1 silver ball clasp
Photo: page 43

Assemble according to the basic pattern at left.

Heavy silver bracelet

FINISHED LENGTH: 7¾" (19 cm)
excluding clasp
MATERIALS:
72 g rings of 14-gauge (2.0 mm) wire, 8 mm ID
1 silver ring clasp, 20 mm
Photo: page 43

Assemble according to the basic pattern. The clasp fastens to the last ring on each end.

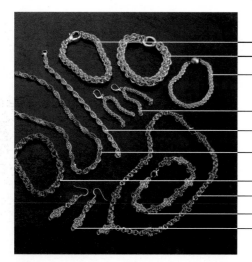

ROPE CHAIN

Key number: 4

To maintain its twist, single rope chain must be re-twisted every time you wear it, or assembled without a clasp in a closed circle.

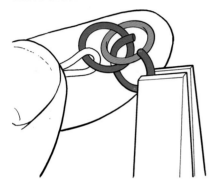

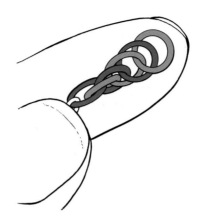

1. Close 1 red ring and place a string or wire in it.
Place a blue ring in it. Lay them flat on your finger overlapping, so that there is a space between them (as shown). Put a red ring in that space.

2. Hold onto the string and turn the top ring so that a handsome, flat pattern emerges.
Set 1 blue ring in the last two rings.
Continue to put 1 ring in the last two rings, rotating the chain as you work to maintain the pattern.

Assembling the chain with no clasp

Rotate (twist) the chain so that the pattern shows throughout the length, lay the ends almost butted up to each other.
Open 1 ring in each end and connect them in a continuation of the pattern.

Silver bracelet

FINISHED LENGTH: 6¾" (17 cm) excluding clasp
MATERIALS:
12 g silver rings, 20-gauge (1.0 mm) wire, 4 mm ID
1 silver clasp, 11 mm, to be mounted directly on the chain
Photo: page 43

Assemble accordingly.

Long necklace in copper and silver

FINISHED LENGTH: 23½" (60 cm) joined without clasp
MATERIALS:
21 g silver rings and 21 g copper rings, both 20-gauge (1.0 mm) wire and 4 mm ID
Photo: page 43

Start with 7 silver rings assembled according to the basic pattern on this page. Alternate 7 silver and 7 copper rings until you reach the desired length.

When joining the two ends, take care that the color and the pattern match perfectly.

DOUBLE ROPE CHAIN

Key number: 5

This rope chain holds its twist quite well without constant re-twisting.

Follow the directions for the basic rope chain (page 44), but use 2 rings instead of 1 in each link.

Copper bracelet

FINISHED LENGTH: 7½″ (18 cm)
  excluding clasp
MATERIALS:
20 g copper rings, 20-gauge (1.0 mm)
  wire, 5 mm ID
1 clasp, 13 mm
Photo: page 43

Assemble this according to the basic pattern for Double Rope chain.

CROSS CHAIN

Key number: 3.5

1. Close 2 red rings and put them on a wire or piece of string.
Join on 2 blue rings, and in these, 2 red rings.

2. Turn the last 2 red rings back, and divide the 2 blue rings. Set 2 blue rings on the turned back red rings and spread them apart.

3. Set 2 red rings in each of the last blue rings and 1 blue in each red pair.

4. Open a blue ring. Pivot the last 2 blue rings back on the red rings. Separate each pair of red rings and, laying the open blue ring flat between them, catch the inside of each of the 2 blue rings. This is the center of the cross figure.

5. Pinch the cross in the middle to make sure the rings are aligned. Put a blue ring in each side through the top 2 red rings, then 2 red rings together through these and 2 blue through the red. Fold these (blue) back, open the latest 2 reds and set 2 red rings through the blue, as shown.

One cross figure consists of 23 rings.

NOTE: Cross chain is so named because it forms a cross in each segment.

Silver and copper necklace

FINISHED LENGTH: 16¾" (42 cm)
excluding clasp
MATERIALS:
26 g copper rings in 20-gauge (1.0 mm)
wire, 4 mm ID
12 g silver rings, 20-gauge (1.0 mm)
wire, 4 mm ID
1 copper clasp, 13 mm
2 copper rings, 18-gauge (1.2 mm) wire,
4 mm ID, for mounting the clasp
Photo: page 43

Assemble according to the basic pattern
on the facing page.

1. Make one copper cross and link it to
a 2-in-2 chain, 9 links long. Use alternating pairs of copper and silver rings. Keep
all the copper rings on the same side.

Repeat step **1** three times.

2. Now you've reached the center of
the chain at 8⅛ inches (20.5 cm). Make
another chain like it.

3. Lay the 2 chains next to each other
and determine that they are the same
length.

4. Make another cross, this time in silver, and join it to the 2 chains with 2
rings on each side at the top of cross.

5. Set the heavier copper rings in each
end of the chain and mount the clasp
on one.

Silver and copper bracelet

FINISHED LENGTH: 7½" (18 cm)
excluding clasp
MATERIALS:
12 g copper rings and 12 g silver rings,
both of 20-gauge (1.0 mm) wire and
3.5 mm ID
1 copper clasp, 13 mm
2 copper rings, 18-gauge (1.2 mm) wire,
4 mm ID to mount the clasp
Photo: page 43

Assemble according to the basic pattern
on facing page.

The bracelet consists of alternating copper and silver crosses—10 in all. When
changing metals, use the last 2 rings of
the existing cross as the first 2 rings in
the new cross. End the chain with a
heavy ring at both ends. Set the clasp in
one of these.

Silver and copper earrings

MATERIALS:
2 silver ear wires
7 g silver rings and 2 g copper rings,
20-gauge (1.0 mm) wire, 3.5 mm ID
Photo: page 43

Assemble according to the basic pattern
on the facing page.

Make 1 cross in silver. Continue with
2-in-2 chain with 1 copper and 1 silver
ring in each link, in all 6 links. Mount
the ear wire in the last one.

The other earring is identical.

JENS PIND'S LINKAGE

Key number: 3

1. Close 1 red ring and thread a string or wire through it.
Set 1 blue ring in the first link, then 1 red through both, turning the last one crosswise.

2. In the crossing that appears with the last 2 rings, set a blue ring. Lay the chain flat.

3. Rotate the chain a half turn and set a red ring inside the last 2 rings.

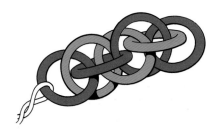

Repeat step **3.**

Dangle earrings

FINISHED LENGTH: 2″ (5 cm)
MATERIALS:
2 closed silver ear wires
14 g rings of 20-gauge (1.0 mm) wire, 3 mm ID
Photo: page 43

Save 2 rings at the end.
Assemble two chains 2 inches (5 cm) long and two chains 1⅝ inches (4 cm) long in the basic pattern.
Join one chain of 1⅝ inch (4 cm) and one 2 inch (5 cm) chain with one of the remaining rings and mount it on the ear wire. Do the same with the remaining two chains.

Silver bracelet

FINISHED LENGTH: 7½″ (18 cm)
excluding clasp
MATERIALS:
57 g rings of 14-gauge (2.0 mm) wire, 6 mm ID
1 silver watch chain fastener, 25 mm
Photo: page 43

Join rings in the basic pattern until you reach the correct length. Mount the fastener directly on the last rings.

SNAKE CHAIN

Key number: 5

This chain is very difficult to start, but easy once it gets going. Particularly for this pattern, it's a good idea to start out with two different metals until you get the feel of it.

Until the first 12 rings are on the chain, use your left thumb and index finger to hold onto the rings. Close the rings with your left thumb and index finger and the help of pliers held in your right hand.

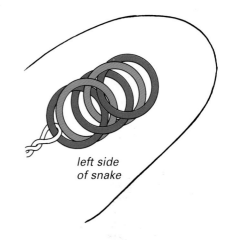

right side
of snake

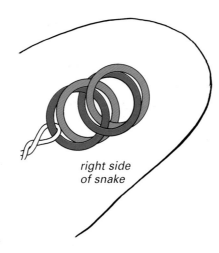

left side
of snake

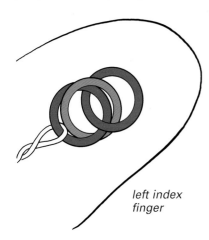

left index
finger

1. Open 6 blue and 6 red rings so they're ready to use.
Close 1 red ring and thread it onto a string or a wire.
Set a blue ring through it.
Set a red ring into the first two. Close this ring. Turn it crosswise to the two first rings. If you drop them, you will have to start over.

2. Set 1 blue ring into the right from the backside into the 2 red rings (but not in the blue, which lies between). Hold on tight! Close the blue ring. Flip it in over the rings so the chain looks "flat". Keep holding on and turn the chain completely over.

3. From the back on the left side, set 1 red ring in the top blue rings (but not in the red one that lies between them). Flip it in over the rings so the chain looks flat. Keep a good hold on everything and turn the chain over again.

Repeat steps **2** and **3**.

Tip: Always put new rings in ring numbers 1 and 3 from the right, and always in the opposite color.

The snake chain pattern develops very clearly when the chain is laid flat. When 12 rings are in place, stop and tidy up the ring closures with pliers.

Silver necklace with heart clasp

FINISHED LENGTH: 16¾" (42 cm)
excluding clasp
MATERIALS:
42 g silver rings of 20-gauge (1.0 mm)
wire, 5 mm ID
1 large, silver heart clasp
2 silver rings of 18-gauge (1.2 mm) wire,
4 mm ID, to attach the clasp
Photo: page 51

Assemble following the basic pattern for
Snake Chain on page 49.

Silver bracelet with heart clasp

FINISHED LENGTH: 7½" (18 cm)
excluding clasp

MATERIALS:
40 g silver rings, 16-gauge (1.5 mm)
wire with 7.5 mm ID
1 large silver heart clasp, attached by
1 ring on each end
Photo: page 51

Assemble according to the basic pattern
for Snake Chain on page 49.

Silver and copper bracelet

FINISHED LENGTH: 6¾" (17 cm)
excluding clasp
MATERIALS:
9 g copper rings and 9 g silver rings,
both of 20-gauge (1.0 mm) wire
with 5 mm ID
1 silver heart clasp
2 silver rings of 18-gauge (1.2 mm) wire,
4 mm ID to attach the clasp
Photo: page 51

Assemble according to the basic pattern
for Snake Chain on preceding page.

The pattern appears when you use 1
silver ring placed in 2 copper rings, and
1 copper ring placed in 2 silver rings.

Heavy silver bracelet

FINISHED LENGTH: 7¾" (19 cm)
excluding clasp
MATERIALS:
73 g rings of 14-gauge (2.0 mm) wire
with 10 mm ID
1 oval ring clasp, which will be attached
to the last ring on each end of the
chain.
Photo: page 51

Assemble following the basic pattern for
Snake Chain on preceding page.

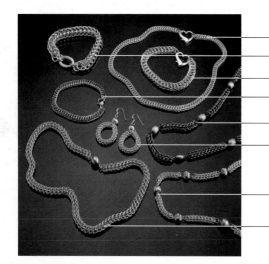

Silver snake necklace with heart clasp p. 50

Heavy silver snake bracelet p. 50

Silver snake bracelet with heart clasp p. 50

Silver and copper snake bracelet p. 50

Oxidized foxtail necklace with silver beads p. 53

Foxtail earrings with silver beads p. 53

Fine foxtail necklace with silver beads p. 53

Foxtail necklace with bead clasp p. 52

FOXTAIL

Key number: 5 or 5.2

For this pattern, you'll need the help of a needle.

1. Close 2 red rings and put them on a string or wire holder, set in the 2 red rings, 2 blue rings and in the blue, 2 red, 2-in-2. Open 2 blue rings.

2. Keeping a firm hold on the first red rings, pull both the blue and red rings to the left, sliding the second red rings to the outside of the first.

3. Now slide the needle into the hole under one red ring, making it stand upright. Then separate the 2 blue rings, slip the needle under the 2 first red rings (with the blue rings still separated), and then under the last red ring, which is also upright.
Leave the needle in place while you insert one blue ring, as shown above.

Remove the needle, and place another blue ring in the same place.

4. Put 2 red rings in the last blue rings on the outside of the second set of red rings.

Repeat steps **3** and **4**.

Necklace with bead clasp

FINISHED LENGTH: 17″ (43 cm)
  excluding findings
MATERIALS:
62 g rings of 20-gauge (1.0 mm) wire,
  5.2 mm ID
1 silver bead clasp
Photo: page 51

Assemble the chain following the basic pattern on this page.

Oxidized necklace with silver beads

FINISHED LENGTH: 17¾" (45 cm) excluding findings
MATERIALS:
53 g silver rings in 20-gauge (1.0 mm) wire with 5 mm ID
6 oval 10 mm corrugated silver beads
7½" (18 cm) 20-gauge (1.0 mm) silver wire
2 silver rings of 20-gauge (1.0 mm) wire, 3.5 mm ID for mounting clasp
1 oval matte silver bead clasp, 9 mm
Photo: page 51

With the rings, assemble 7 segments, each 2 inches (5 cm) long, following the basic Foxtail pattern on the facing page.
Cut the 7½ inch (18 cm) silver wire into 1⅛-inch (3 cm) pieces.

Put each bead on a piece of wire and use round-nose pliers to form an eye on each end. The Foxtail segments will be mounted on these.

Join the 7 segments with beads. End with a single ring in each end of the chain. Mount the bead clasp and when finished, oxidize the necklace (see page 6).

Fine necklace with silver beads

FINISHED LENGTH: 16¼" (41 cm) excluding findings
MATERIALS:
30 g silver rings of 22-gauge (0.8 mm) wire, 4 mm ID
1 silver ball clasp
8 corrugated silver beads, 7 mm
9⅜" (24 cm) 22-gauge (0.8 mm) silver wire
2 rings in 20-gauge (1.0 mm) wire, 3.5 mm ID
Photo: page 51

Assemble 9 segments, each 1⅛ inch (3 cm) long, following the basic pattern for Foxtail on facing page.
Cut the silver wire into 1-inch (2.5 cm) pieces.
String these pieces through the beads and make a little eye at each end (see drawing to left).
Assemble beads and Foxtail segments.
Mount the clasp with 1 ring on each side.

Earrings with silver beads

MATERIALS:
15 g silver rings in 22-gauge (0.8 mm) wire with 4 mm ID
2 corrugated silver beads, 7 mm
2⅜" (6 cm) 22-gauge (0.8 mm) silver wire
2 silver ear wires
Photo: page 51

Assemble a 2⅝ inch (7 cm) chain following the basic Foxtail pattern on the facing page.
Cut wire in half, and mount 1 bead on each wire, bending the wire into eyes at each end. Mount the chain on one eye and the ear wire on the other.
Make another.

BYZANTINE CHAIN

Key number: 3.5

In Byzantine chain, you always build on the last 2 rings inserted.

1. Close 2 red rings and put them on a wire or string holder.

2. Put 2 blue in the 2 first red rings and then 2 red in the blue, 2-in-2.

3. Flip the last 2 red rings back so they lie against the first red rings.
Separate the blue rings.
Push the flipped red rings forward and set 2 blue rings in the red rings between the blue.

4. Put 2 red rings on the blue rings, then 2 blue on those. Flip the 2 blue backward and up, then divide the red, and push the 2 blue forward a little.

5. Put 2 red rings between the parted red rings and into the flipped back blue rings. The first segment is finished.

If the chain is to be a single piece, repeat steps **2** through **5**.

Silver necklace

FINISHED LENGTH: 16½" (42 cm)
excluding findings
MATERIALS:
46 g silver rings of 20-gauge (1.0 mm) wire with 3.5 mm ID
1 silver clasp, 11 mm
Photo: page 57

Assemble accordingly.

Necklace with clasp

FINISHED LENGTH: 15⅜" (39 cm)
excluding findings
MATERIALS:
30 g silver rings of 22-gauge (0.8 mm) wire with 3 mm ID
1 silver heart clasp
Photo: page 57

Assemble according to the basic pattern for Byzantine chain on this page.

Silver roll-on chain bracelet

FINISHED LENGTH: 8³⁄₈″ (21 cm)
MATERIALS:
35 g silver rings of 16-gauge (1.5 mm)
    wire, 5 mm ID
7 silver rings (7 g) in 14-gauge (2.0 mm)
    wire, 7 mm ID
Photo: page 54

Assemble the small rings into 6 segments of Byzantine chain following the basic pattern on page 54.

Use the large rings to join the segments.

Silver pendant on leather cord

MATERIALS:
15 silver rings (about 3 g) of 18-gauge
    (1.2 mm) wire with 4 mm ID
31¼″ (80 cm) 2 mm black leather cord
Photo: page 57

Assemble following the basic Byzantine chain pattern on page 54.

Make 1 segment of 14 rings and set the last ring in one end. Thread the leather through this ring and tie sliding knots (see page 12).

Silver brooch and tie guard

MATERIALS:
7 g silver rings of 20-gauge (1.0 mm)
    wire, 3.5 mm ID
Brooch: 1 silvered stickpin, with
    hook 180 mm
Tie guard: about 6¼″ (16 cm)
    20-gauge (1.0 mm) silver wire
Photo: page 57

The chain:
Assemble according to the Byzantine chain directions on page 54.
Make 4 segments.

Join the segments with 1 ring between. Place a single ring in each end of the finished chain to attach to the pin or tie guard.

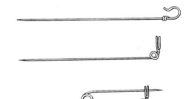

Make the pin with round-nose pliers
1. Turn the hook at the head of the pin up at a right angle with the pliers and make a little eye around the tip of the pliers

2. Measure 2¾ inches (7 cm) from the point and bend the pin around the pliers, so that the pin looks like a V, with one side 2¾ inches (7 cm) long.

3. Keep bending the side with the head until it forms a spring eye and touches the other leg.

Tie guard hanger
Form the hanger with round-nose pliers as described on page 28.

Oxidized bracelet with twisted rings

FINISHED LENGTH: 6¾″ (17 cm)
    excluding findings
MATERIALS:
25 g silver rings of 18-gauge (1.2 mm)
    wire, 4 mm ID
24 twisted rings made from 3′ 4½″
    (1 m) of 24-gauge (0.6 mm) wire on
    a 4 mm mandrel (see pages 30-31).
1 clasp
Photo: page 57

Assemble according to the basic pattern for Byzantine chain on preceding page.

1. Close 2 smooth rings and set 2 smooth rings into them, 2-in-2.

2. Set into these 1 smooth and 1 twisted ring.

3. Flip the last 2 rings and set in them 1 smooth and 1 twisted ring.

4. Into this set 1 smooth and 1 twisted ring.

5. Set 2 smooth rings into this. Flip them and finish with 2 smooth rings (following the basic pattern all the way). Keep the twisted rings on the same side throughout.

6. Assemble 8 segments like this, connect them with smooth rings, and end with a smooth ring in each end. Mount the clasp on one end.

Tapered silver necklace

FINISHED LENGTH: 11" (28 cm)
excluding findings
MATERIALS:
1 silver ring clasp, 20 mm
A: 234 silver rings (24 g) of 20-gauge (1.0 mm) wire, 3.5 mm ID
B: 38 rings (9 g) of 18-gauge (1.2 mm) wire, 4 mm ID
C: 26 rings (8 g) of 16-gauge (1.5 mm) wire, 5 mm ID
D: 10 rings (10 g) in 14-gauge (2.0 mm) wire, 7 mm ID
Photo: page 57

Assemble according to the basic Byzantine chain pattern on page 54.

Assemble 14 segments with A rings.

Link them together with B rings into 2 chains, each 7 segments long, and end with a B ring.

Following the basic pattern, build from this B ring to make the center section, using, in this order:

14 A rings
12 B rings
12 C rings
10 D rings
12 C rings
12 B rings
14 A rings

Set a B ring in the last link and join it to the second 7-segment section.

End the chain with a C ring at each end and insert the ring clasp in these.

Tapered dangle earrings

MATERIALS:
2 silver ear wires
A: 26 rings (4 g) of 20-gauge (1.0 mm) wire, 3.5 mm ID
B: 28 rings (6 g) of 18-gauge (1.2 mm) wire, 4 mm ID
Photo: page 57

Assemble according to the basic Byzantine chain pattern on page 54.

Assemble a segment of B rings, then continue with 12 A rings and end with 1 A ring. Set the ear wire in the last A ring.

Make another just like it.

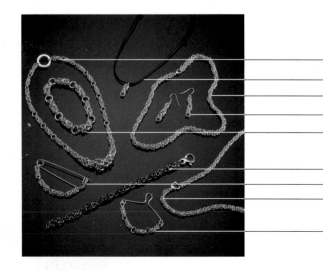

Tapered Byzantine silver necklace p. 56
Silver Byzantine pendant on leather cord p. 55

Silver Byzantine necklace p. 54
Tapered Byzantine dangle earrings p. 56
Silver roll-on bracelet in Byzantine chain p. 55

Oxidized Byzantine bracelet with twisted rings p. 55
Silver Byzantine brooch p. 55
Silver Byzantine chain necklace with heart clasp p. 54

Silver Byzantine tie guard p. 55

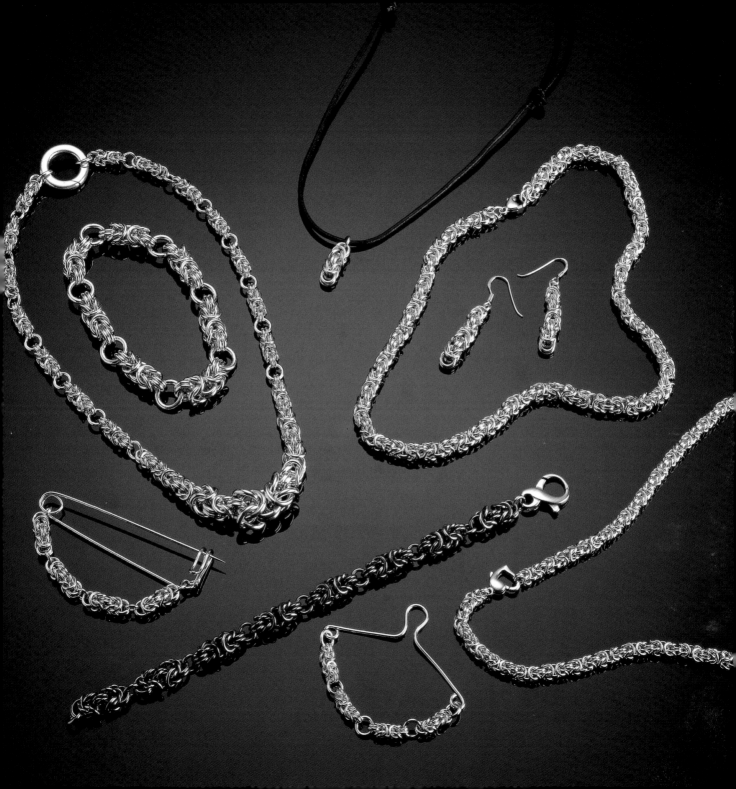

SUPPLIERS AND TOOLS

Materials needed to complete the projects in this book may be available at local craft stores or bead and jewelry shops. In addition, the following mail-order companies offer tools and supplies for metal-working and jewelry-making.

USA

ARE Supply Company
636 11th Avenue South
Hopkins, MN 55343
(800) 736-4273
(612) 912-0982
Fax: (612) 912-0981

Bourget Brothers
1636 11th Street
Santa Monica, CA 90404
(800) 828-3024
(310) 450-6556

Frei & Borel
P.O. Box 796
126 Second Street
Oakland, CA 94604
(800) 772-3456
(415) 832-0355
Fax: (415) 834-6217

Paul Gesswein and Co., Inc.
255 Hancock Avenue
P.O. Box 3998
Bridgeport, CT 06605-0936
(800) 243-4466
(203) 366-5400
Fax: (203) 366-3953
Website:
www.gessweinco.com

T.B. Hagstoz & Son
709 Sansom Street
Philadelphia, PA 19106
(800) 922-1006
(215) 922-1627
Fax: (215) 922-7126

Rio Grande Albuquerque
7500 Bluewater Road, NW
Albuquerque, NM 87121
from USA (800) 545-6566
from Canada or Mexico (800) 253-9738
Fax: (505) 821-5529
Website: www.riogrande.com

Australia

Kodak Jeweler's Supplies
4th Floor Century Building
125 Swanston Street
Melbourne, Victoria 3000
(03) 9654 5811
Fax: (03) 9650 1835

Canada

Gesswein (Canada) Ltd.
317 Attwell Drive
Rexdale, Ontario M9W 5C1
(800) 263-6106
(416) 675-9171
Tools only

Lacy and Co. Ltd.
291 Yonge Street
Toronto, Ontario M5B 1R3
(416) 979-8383
E-mail: lacy-on.aibn.com

United Kingdom

J. Blundell & Sons Ltd.
199 Wardour Street
London W1V 4JN
(01) 71 437 4746

J.K. Tools & Findings
58g Hatton Garden
London EC1N 8LS
(01) 71 404 0563

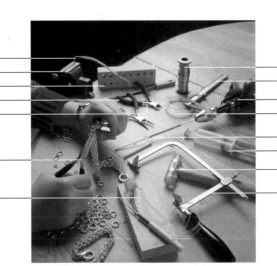

Mandrel holding Viking knit project
Mini-vise
Drawplate
File
Nippers (right) and round-nose pliers (left)

Flat-nose pliers

Jig for knitting on 3 nails, with knitting

Copper wire
Vernier gauge (for measuring)
Hand drill
Silver wire

Mandrel with spiral of copper wire
2-component epoxy glue

Plastic hammer

Jeweler's saw

INSIDE DIAMETERS (ID)

The key number times the *metric* gauge of the wire yields the mandrel size (rounded off in the chart).

KEY NUMBER	WIRE					
	24-gauge 0.6 mm	22-gauge 0.8 mm	20-gauge 1.0 mm	18-gauge 1.2 mm	16-gauge 1.5 mm	14-gauge 2.0 mm
3.0	2.0	2.5	3.0	3.5	4.5	6.0
3.5	2.0	3.0	3.5	4.0	5.0	7.0
4.0	unsuitable	3.0	4.0	5.0	6.0	8.0
5.0	unsuitable	4.0	5.0	6.0	7.5	10.0
5.2	unsuitable	4.5	5.2/5.5	6.5	8.0	10.5

Knitting Needle Metric Conversions

U.S. SIZE	0	1	2	3	4	5	6	7	8	9	10	10.5
METRIC SIZE (mm)	2	2.25	2.5	3	3.5	3.75	4	4.25	5	5.5	6	7

INDEX